MATH
INSTANT ASSESSMENTS
for Data Tracking
Kindergarten

Credits
Author: Jeanette Moore, MS Ed.

Visit *carsondellosa.com* for correlations to Common Core, state, national, and Canadian provincial standards.

Carson-Dellosa Publishing, LLC
PO Box 35665
Greensboro, NC 27425 USA
carsondellosa.com

978-1-4838-3597-6
01-339161151

Table of Contents

Assessment and Data Tracking

Data tracking is an essential element in modern classrooms. Teachers are often required to capture student learning through both formative and summative assessments. They then must use the results to guide teaching, remediation, and lesson planning and provide feedback to students, parents, and administrators. Because time is always at a premium in the classroom, it is vital that teachers have the assessments they need at their fingertips. The assessments need to be suited to the skill being assessed as well as adapted to the stage in the learning process. This is true for an informal checkup at the end of a lesson or a formal assessment at the end of a unit.

This book will provide the tools and assessments needed to determine your students' level of mastery throughout the school year. The assessments are both formal and informal and include a variety of formats—pretests and posttests, flash cards, prompt cards, traditional tests, and exit tickets. Often, there are several assessment options for a single skill or concept to allow you the greatest flexibility when assessing understanding. Simply select the assessment that best fits your needs, or use them all to create a comprehensive set of assessments for before, during, and after learning.

Incorporate Instant Assessments into your daily plans to streamline the data-tracking process and keep the focus on student mastery and growth.

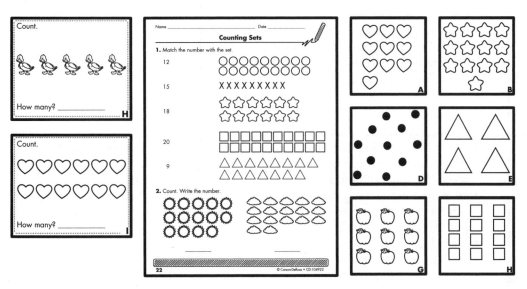

A variety of instant assessments for counting sets

Types of Assessment

Assessment usually has a negative association because it brings to mind tedious pencil-and-paper tests and grading. However, it can take on many different forms and be a positive, integral part of the year. Not all assessments need to be formal, nor do they all need to be graded. Choose the type of assessment to use based on the information you need to gather. Then, you can decide if or how it should be graded.

	What Does It Look Like?	Examples
Formative Assessment	• occurs during learning • is administered frequently • is usually informal and not graded • identifies areas of improvement • provides immediate feedback so a student can make adjustments promptly, if needed • allows teachers to rethink strategies, lesson content, etc., based on current student performance • is process-focused • has the most impact on a student's performance	• in-class observations • exit tickets • reflections and journaling • homework • student-teacher conferences • student self-evaluations
Interim Assessment	• occurs occasionally • is more formal and usually graded • feedback is not immediate, though still fairly quick • helps teachers identify gaps in teaching and areas for remediation • often includes performance assessments, which are individualized, authentic, and performance-based in order to evaluate higher-level thinking skills	• in-class observations • exit tickets • reflections and journaling • homework • student-teacher conferences • student self-evaluations
Summative Assessment	• occurs once learning is considered complete • the information is used by the teacher and school for broader purposes • takes time to return a grade or score • can be used to compare a student's performance to others • is product-focused • has the least impact on a student's performance since there are few or no opportunities for retesting	• cumulative projects • final portfolios • quarterly testing • end-of-the-year testing • standardized testing

How to Use This Book

The assessments in this book follow a few different formats, depending on the skill or concept being assessed. Use the descriptions below to familiarize yourself with each unique format and get the most out of Instant Assessments all year long.

Show What You Know
Each domain begins with a pair of *Show What You Know* tests. Both tests follow the same format and include the same types of questions so they can be directly compared to show growth. Use them as a pretest and posttest. Or, use one as a test at the end of a unit and use the second version as a retest for students after remediation.

Exit Tickets
Each domain ends with exit tickets that cover the variety of concepts within the domain. Exit tickets are very targeted questions designed to assess understanding of specific skills, so they are ideal formative assessments to use at the end of a lesson. Exit tickets do not have space for student names, allowing teachers to gather information on the entire class without placing pressure on individual students. If desired, have students write their names or initials on the backs of the tickets. Other uses for exit tickets include the following:

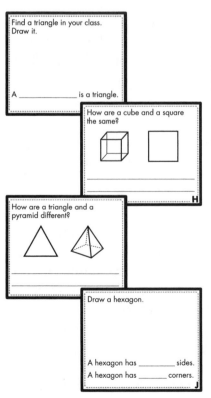

- Use the back of each ticket for longer answers, fuller explanations, or extension questions. If needed, students can staple them to larger sheets of paper.
- They can also be used for warm-ups or to find out what students know before a lesson.
- Use the generic exit tickets on pages 7 and 8 for any concept you want to assess. Be sure to fill in any blanks before copying.
- Laminate them and place them in a math center as task cards.
- Use them to play Scoot or a similar review game at the end of a unit.
- Choose several to create a targeted assessment for a skill or set of skills.

Cards

Use the cards as prompts for one-on-one conferencing. Simply copy the cards, cut them apart, and follow the directions preceding each set of cards. Use the lettering to keep track of which cards a student has interacted with.

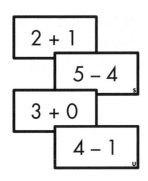

- Copy on card stock and/or laminate for durability.
- Punch holes in the top left corners and place the cards on a book ring to make them easily accessible.
- Copy the sets on different colors of paper to keep them easily separated or to distinguish different sections within a set of cards.
- Easily differentiate by using different amounts or levels of cards to assess a student.
- Write the answers on the backs of cards to create self-checking flash cards.
- Place them in a math center as task cards or matching activities.
- Use them to play Scoot or a similar review game at the end of a unit.

Assessment Pages

The reproducible assessment pages are intended for use as a standard test of a skill. Use them in conjunction with other types of assessment to get a full picture of a student's level of understanding. They can also be used for review or homework.

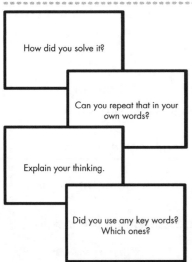

Math Talk Prompt Cards

Use the math talk prompt cards on pages 9 and 10 to prompt math discussions that can be used to informally assess students' levels of understanding. Use the math talk prompts to encourage reflection and deeper understanding of math concepts throughout the year.

- Copy on card stock and/or laminate for durability.
- Punch holes in the top left corners and place the cards on a book ring to keep them easily accessible.
- Use them for journaling prompts.
- Place them in a math center to be used with other activities.

Exit Tickets

Exit tickets are a useful formative assessment tool that you can easily work into your day. You can choose to use a single exit ticket at the end of the day or at the end of each lesson. Simply choose a ticket below and make one copy for each student. Then, have students complete the prompt and present them to you as their ticket out of the door. Use the student responses to gauge overall learning, create small remediation groups, or target areas for reteaching. A blank exit ticket is included on page 8 so you can create your own exit tickets as well.

What stuck with you today?

_____

_____

_____

List three facts you learned today. Put them in order from most important to least important.

1. _____

2. _____

3. _____

The first thing I'll tell my family about today is

_____

_____

_____

_____

The most important thing I learned today is

_____

_____

_____

Color the face that shows how you feel about understanding today's lesson.

Explain why. _____

_____

Summarize today's lesson in 10 words or less.

_____

_____

_____

_____

One example of _____ is _____

_____

_____

_____ .

One question I still have is _____

_____

_____

_____ .

How will understanding _____

_____

help you in real life? _____

_____

_____

One new word I learned today is

_____ .

It means _____

_____

_____ .

Draw a picture related to the lesson. Add a caption.

_____

_____

If today's lesson were a song, the title would be _____

_____

because _____

_____ .

The answer is _____ .

What is the question? _____

_____

_____

_____

Math Talk Prompts

Use these prompts when observing individual students in order to better understand their thinking and depth of understanding of a concept. These cards may also be used during whole-class lessons or in small remediation groups to encourage students to explain their thinking with different concepts.

How did you solve it?	What strategy did you use?
How could you solve it a different way?	Can you repeat that in your own words?
Explain your thinking.	Did you use any key words? Which ones?

Can you explain why you chose to do that?	Why did you choose to add/subtract/ multiply/divide?
How do you know your answer is correct?	How can you prove your answer?
Is this like any other problems you have solved? How?	What would change if . . . ?
Why is _____ important?	What do you need to do next? Why?

✦ Show What You Know ✦
Counting and Cardinality

1. Count to 50. Fill in the missing numbers.

1	2		4	5	6		8	9	10
11		13	14	15	16		18	19	
21	22	23	24		26	27	28	29	30
	32	33	34	35	36	37		39	40
41	42	43		45	46		48	49	50

2. Count to 80 by tens. Fill in the missing numbers.

10, _____ , 30, _____ , 50, 60, _____ , 80

3. Write the numbers from 0 to 10.

_____ _____ _____ _____ _____ _____

_____ _____ _____ _____ _____

4. Count the dogs. Write a number under each dog as you count on.

_____   _____   _____   _____   _____

There are _____ dogs in all.

5. Count the cars. Write how many.

_____

6. There were 9 fish in the pond during the day.

There were 11 fish in the pond at night.

There were _____ more fish in the pond at night than in the day.

7. Which set has more? Circle it.

8. Which is more? Circle the number.

3 or 6   9 or 10   17 or 12

Name _____ Date _____

✦ Show What You Know ✦
Counting and Cardinality

1. Count to 70. Fill in the missing numbers.

1		3	4		6	7		9	10
	12	13		15	16		18	19	20
21	22		24	25		27	28		30
31	32	33	34	35	36	37	38	39	
41	42		44	45	46		48	49	50
51	52	53		55	56	57	58	59	60
61	62		64	65	66	67		69	70

2. Count to 100 by tens. Fill in the missing numbers.

10, 20, _____, 40, 50, _____, 70, _____, 90, 100

3. Write the numbers from 0 to 20.

_____ _____ _____ _____ _____ _____ _____

_____ _____ _____ _____ _____ _____ _____

_____ _____ _____ _____ _____ _____ _____

4. Count the ducks. Write a number under each duck as you count on.

_____ _____ _____ _____ _____ _____

There are _____ ducks in all.

5. Count the cats. Write how many.

_____

6. The bush had 8 flowers on Friday.

Then, there were 11 flowers on Sunday.

There were _____ more flowers on Sunday than on Friday.

7. Which set has less cars? Circle it.

8. Which is less? Circle the number.

3 or 5   9 or 8   19 or 9

Number Concepts

Use these cards to assess a student's understanding of a variety of number concepts. Present a card which the student must count to by ones or by tens. Or, have students count on from a number other than 1. Students may also recognize and name a number, create a set to match a number, or compare two numbers from 0–10. To assess place value concepts, present students with a 10 and a number from 1–9 and have him name the number and build it with place value manipulatives. If desired, laminate the task cards for durability, or so students can use write-on/wipe-away markers.

10	20	30
40	50	60
70	80	90

100	0	1
2	3	4
5	6	7
8	9	10

0	1	2
3	4	5
6	7	8
9	10	

Counting

1. Count. Fill in the missing numbers.

1	2		4		6	7	8	9	
11		13	14	15	16	17	18	19	20
21	22		24	25	26		28	29	
31	32	33		35	36	37	38	39	40
	42	43	44	45		47	48	49	50
51	52		54	55	56	57	58	59	
61	62	63		65	66	67		69	70
	72	73	74	75		77	78	79	80
81		83		85	86	87	88		90
91	92	93	94		96	97	98	99	100

2. Look at the chart above. Color the tens blue.

3. Count on.

11, _____, _____, _____, _____, _____

4. Count on.

37, _____, _____, _____, _____, _____

5. What numbers are between 1 and 7?

1, _____, _____, _____, _____, _____, 7

Writing Numbers

Use these cards to assess a student's proficiency with writing numerals and counting sets. Show the student a card and have her count the objects and write the related numeral on a separate sheet of paper. Or, choose several to create a whole-class assessment. You may also present a card and have a student make a matching set, or a set with more or fewer objects. If desired, laminate the cards and allow students to use write-on/wipe away markers to draw on the sets. (Note: Card Q represents zero.)

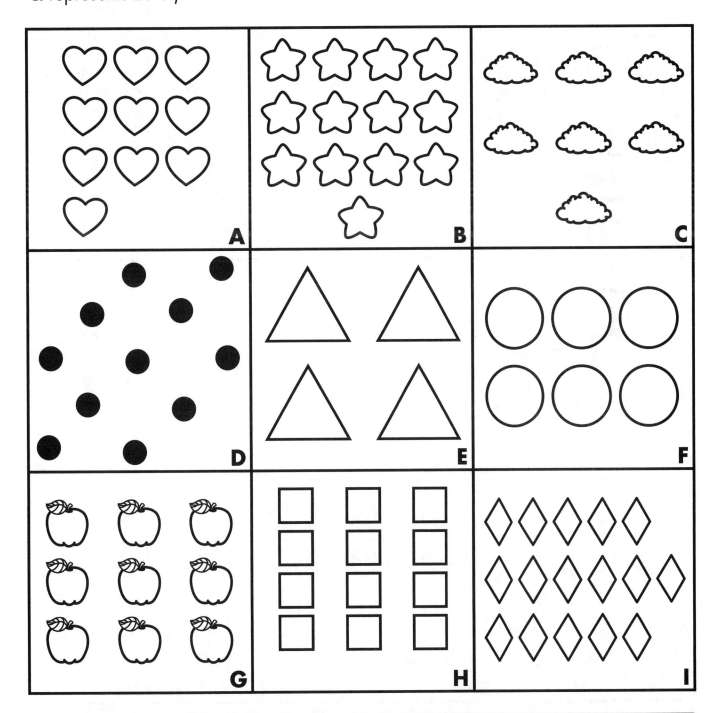

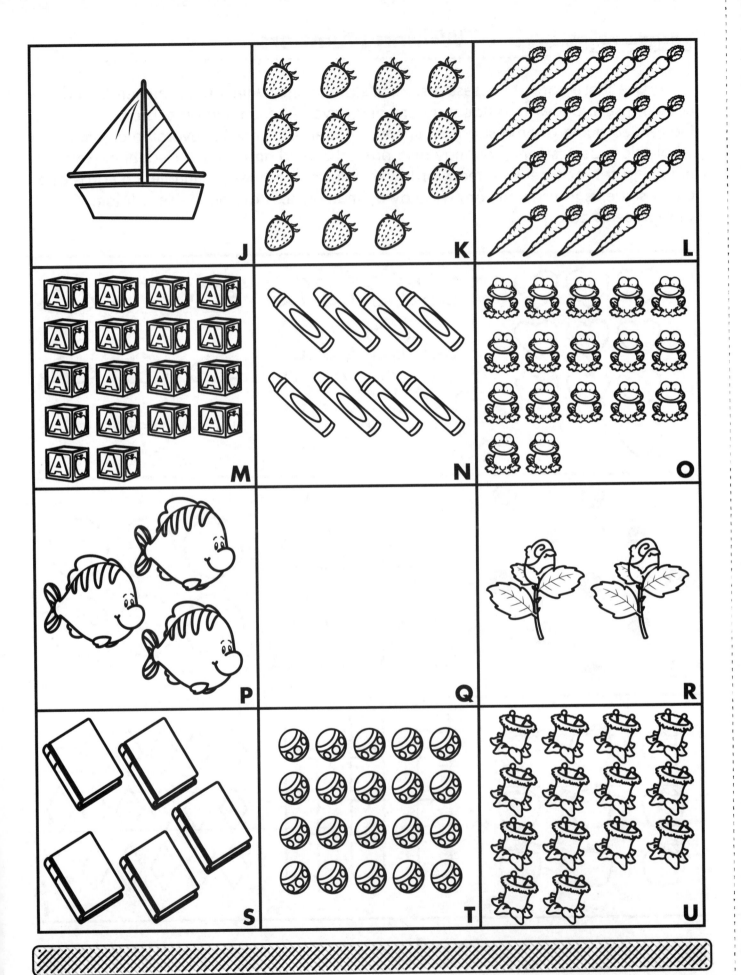

Writing Numbers

Count. Write the number.

1.

_____

2.
_____

3.

_____

4.

_____

Draw a set of dots. Write the number.

5.

_____

Counting Sets

1. Match the number with the set.

12

15

18

20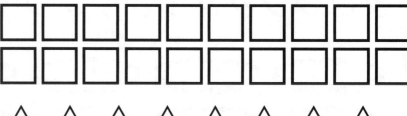

9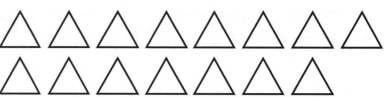

2. Count. Write the number.

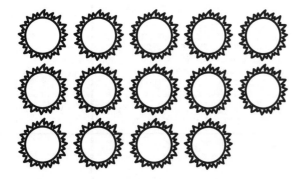   

_____   _____

Counting with Objects

Pick up a handful of counters for each problem.

1. Draw a set of dots to match.

Count. Write how many. _____

2. Draw a set of triangles to match.

Count. Write how many. _____

3. Draw a set of circles to match.

Count. Write how many. _____

4. Draw a set of squares to match.

Count. Write how many. _____

Comparing Sets

Compare each set. Which is greater? Circle it.

1. ♡♡♡♡♡ ♡♡♡♡♡   ♡♡♡♡♡ ♡♡♡

2. ☐☐☐☐☐☐ ☐☐☐☐☐   ☐☐☐☐☐☐☐ ☐☐☐☐☐☐

3. ○○○○○○ ○○   ○○○○○○ ○○○○○

4. 🍎🍎🍎🍎🍎🍎🍎 🍎🍎🍎🍎🍎🍎🍎   🍎🍎🍎🍎🍎 🍎🍎🍎🍎

5. ◇◇◇◇◇◇◇◇ ◇◇◇◇◇◇◇◇   ◇◇◇◇◇◇◇◇◇ ◇◇◇◇◇◇◇◇

6. △△△△△△ △△△△△△   △△△△△△△ △△△△△△△

7. ●●●●● ●●●●   ●●●● ●●●

8. ☆☆☆☆☆☆ ☆☆☆☆☆☆   ☆☆☆☆☆ ☆☆☆☆

Comparing Numbers

Compare the numbers. Circle the number that is less.
Draw an **X** on the the numbers that are equal.

1.   6   4

2.   7   7

3.   6   1

4.   8   8

5.   16   9

6.   10   9

7.   2   0

8.   12   14

9.   6   15

10.   17   19

Comparing Numbers

1. Color the set of shapes with more.

2. Color the set of shapes with less.

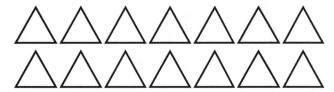 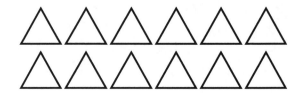

3. Color the sets that are equal.

4. Circle the number that is greater.

7   9

5. Circle the number that is less.

8   10

A

Count by ones. Write the missing numbers.

3, _____ , 5, 6, 7, _____

1, _____ , 3, 4, _____ , 6

B

Count by tens. Color the numbers you say.

1	2	3	4	5	6	7	8	9	10
11	12	13	14	15	16	17	18	19	20
21	22	23	24	25	26	27	28	29	30

C

Count on.

0, _____ , _____ , _____ , _____ , _____

4, _____ , _____ , _____ , _____ , _____

D

Draw 8 cups.

E

Draw 20 blocks.

F

Draw 22 circles.

Count.

How many? _____

G

Count.

How many? _____

H

Count.

How many? _____

I

Circle the number that is greater.

7   10

J

Circle the number that is less.

5   8

K

Circle the group that has more.

L

Name _____ Date _____

1. There are 4 dots and 2 dots. How many dots in all? Draw the dots to solve.

2. Solve.

_____   _____   _____

3. Solve.

_____ − _____ = _____

4. Draw the problem. Then, solve it.   4 − 1 = _____

5. Circle the two facts that add to 5.

$$2 + 3 \qquad 4 + 0 \qquad 1 + 4$$

6. Circle the two facts that equal 7.

$$4 + 3 \qquad 6 + 1 \qquad 5 + 3$$

7. Show ten in all.

How many did you add to show 10? _____

8. Show ten in all.

How many did you add to show 10? _____

✦ Show What You Know ✦
Operations & Algebraic Thinking

1. There are 6 carrots. A bunny eats 3. How many are left? Draw the carrots to solve.

2. Solve.

_____   _____   _____

3. Solve.

_____   –   _____   =   _____

4. Draw the problem. Then, solve it.   6 + 2 = _____

5. Circle the two facts that add to 5.

$3 + 2$ $2 + 0$ $0 + 5$

6. Circle the two facts that equal 9.

$6 + 3$ $1 + 8$ $5 + 1$

7. Show ten in all.

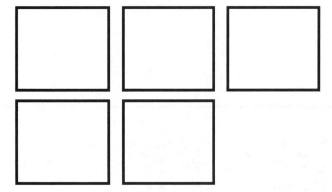

How many did you add to show 10? _____

8. Show ten in all.

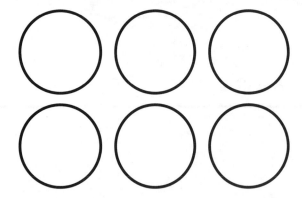

How many did you add to show 10? _____

Patterning

Continue the pattern.

1.  _____ _____

2. 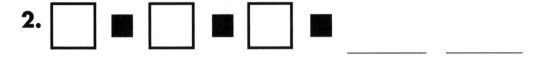 _____ _____

3.  _____ _____ _____

Draw the missing shape in each pattern. Then, tell about the pattern.

4.

_____

_____

5.

_____

_____

Representing Addition and Subtraction

Write a number sentence for each picture.

1.

_____

2.

_____

3.

_____

4.

_____

5.

_____

Representing Addition and Subtraction

Use these cards as prompts for assessing students' understanding of addition and subtraction. Read a prompt aloud to a student. Or, choose several to make a whole-class assessment. Provide a set of small objects (i.e. buttons or paper clips) or have the student use his fingers to represent the addition or subtraction (cards A–L). You may also choose to have him use mental imagery (cards M–R), draw (cards S–X), or act out equations and use sounds (cards Y–AD). For additional insight, have students verbally explain each equation and how they solved it.

Place 4 (objects) on the table. Add 4 more (objects) to the set. Count them. How many (objects) in all? **A**	Place 7 (objects) on the table. Add 3 more (objects) to the set. Count them. How many (objects) in all? **B**
Place 9 (objects) on the table. Add 1 more (object) to the set. Count them. How many (objects) in all? **C**	Place 10 (objects) on the table. Take 4 (objects) away. How many (objects) are left? **D**
Place 5 (objects) on the table. Take 1 (object) away. How many (objects) are left? **E**	Place 8 (objects) on the table. Take 2 (objects) away. How many (objects) are left? **F**

Hold up 5 fingers. Hold up 2 more fingers. How many fingers in all?

G

Hold up 3 fingers. Hold up 2 more fingers. How many fingers in all?

H

Hold up 7 fingers. Hold up 1 more finger. How many fingers in all?

I

Hold up 10 fingers. Put 3 fingers down. How many fingers are left?

J

Hold up 9 fingers. Put 5 fingers down. How many fingers are left?

K

Hold up 7 fingers. Put 3 fingers down. How many fingers are left?

L

Imagine looking for shells on the beach. You find 4. Then, you find 2 more. How many shells in all?

M

Imagine seeing frogs at the pond. You see 3. Then, you see 4 more. How many frogs in all?

N

Imagine collecting rocks. You find 5. Then you find 4 more. How many rocks in all?

O

Picture 9 birds in a tree. Then, 3 fly away. How many birds are left?

P

Picture 8 ducks in the pond. Then, 4 swim away. How many ducks are left?

Q

Picture 5 ladybugs on a leaf. Then, 5 of them crawl away. How many ladybugs are left?

R

Draw a picture that shows 2 groups of 3 friends. How many friends in all?

S

Draw a picture that shows 2 groups of 4 spiders. How many spiders in all?

T

Draw a picture that shows 2 groups of 5 flowers. How many flowers in all?

U

Draw 7 clouds. Two clouds disappear. How many clouds are left?

V

Draw 8 lollipops. Some friends eat 4 of the lollipops. How many lollipops are left?

W

Draw 9 balls. Then, 5 balls get lost. How many balls are left?

X

Raise 1 hand. Raise the other hand. How many hands in all?

Y

Take 1 step forward. Take 2 more steps forward. How many steps in all?

Z

Tap your foot 3 times. Tap your foot 4 more times. How many taps in all?

AA

Clap your hands 5 times. Clap your hands 3 more times. How many claps in all?

AB

Tap the table gently 2 times. Tap the table 2 more times. How many taps in all?

AC

Say your name 3 times. Say it once more. How many times did you say your name?

AD

Addition Word Problems

Solve. Draw a picture to help you.

1. Dom put 7 toys in the toy box. There are 2 more toys to put away. How many toys are there in all?

2. John ate 2 snacks in the morning. Then, he ate 1 snack after lunch. How many snacks did he eat in all?

3. Maya fed the dog 2 times on Monday. She fed him 2 times on Tuesday. How many times did she feed him in all?

4. Mel put 4 socks in the box. Then, she put 4 more in. How many in all?

Name _____ Date _____

Subtraction Word Problems

Solve. Draw a picture to help you.

1. Ian had 3 toy boats in his bath. He took 1 boat out of the water. How many boats were left in the water?

2. Lu bought 6 bananas. He ate 1 banana. How many were left?

3. Will had 7 trucks. He gave 2 trucks to his friend. How many trucks did he have left?

4. Cora had 4 books to read. She took 2 books back to the library. How many are left to read?

Decomposing Numbers to 10

Use two colors to color each set of cubes a different way.

1. There are four ways to make 3. Show each way.

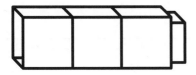   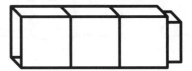

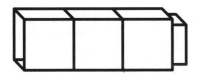   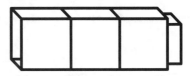

2. There are five ways to make 4. Show each way.

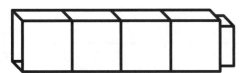   

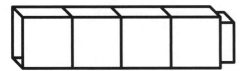   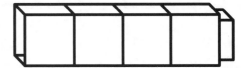

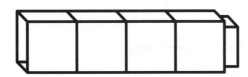

Decomposing Numbers to 10

There are eight ways to make 7. Use two colors to color each set of stripes a different way. Then, write the math fact shown on each scarf.

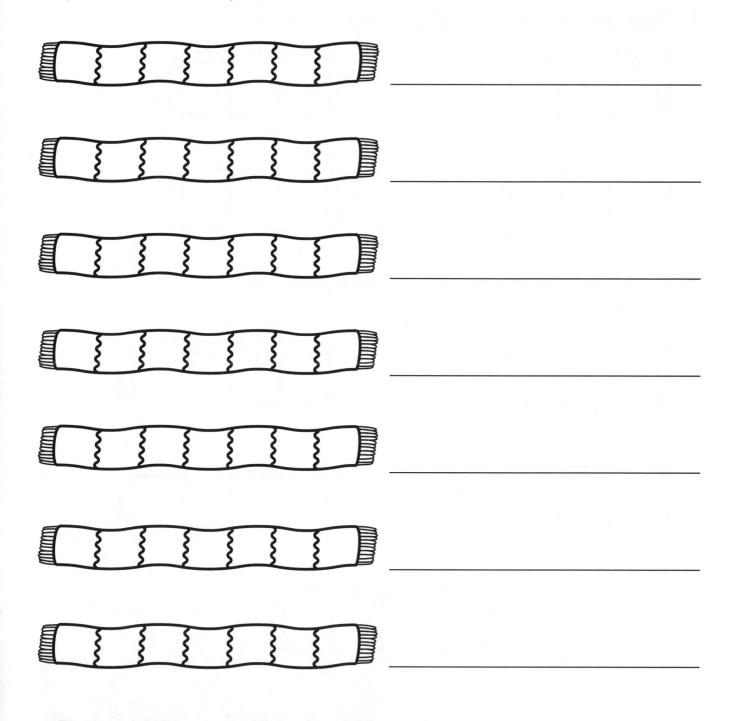

Decomposing Numbers to 10

Write the related fact for each cube train.

1.

_____ + _____ = _____

2.

_____ + _____ = _____

3. Write each missing number.

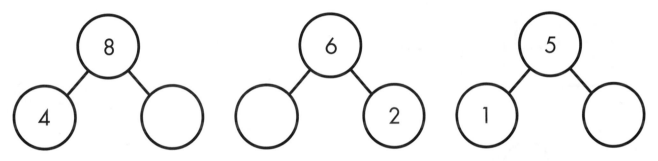

4. Draw an **X** on the facts that do not add to 6.

1 + 5	3 + 4	3 + 3
2 + 4	2 + 3	4 + 1

5. How many ways can you make 4? Draw or write facts.

Making 10

Add shapes to make a set of 10. Then, tell how many shapes you added.

1.

_____ more

2.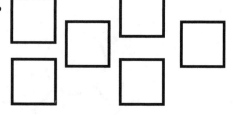

_____ more

3.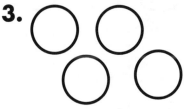

_____ more

4.

_____ more

5.

_____ more

Making 10

Write the missing number to make 10.

1.
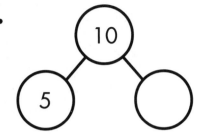

2.
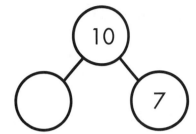

3.
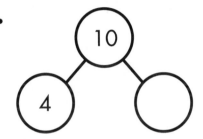

4.
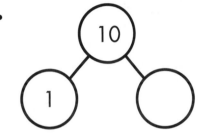

5.
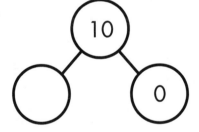

6.
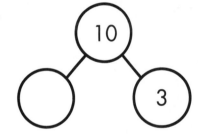

7.
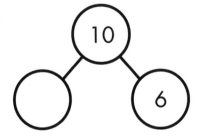

8.
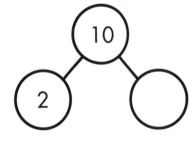

9.
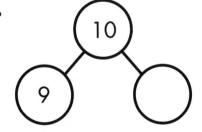

10.
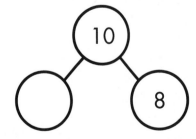

Name _____ Date _____

Making 10

Write the missing number.

1. _____ + 6 = 10

2. 2 + _____ = 10

3. 0 + _____ = 10

4. _____ + 5 = 10

5. _____ + 3 = 10

6. _____ + 9 = 10

7. 8 + _____ = 10

8. 10 + _____ = 10

9. _____ + 7 = 10

10. 1 + _____ = 10

Addition and Subtraction within Five

Use the fact cards to assess students' fluency with addition and subtraction facts within five. Place cards into piles based on a student's response. The first pile should contain facts the student answered quickly and correctly. The second pile should contain facts the student answered with hesitation, but correctly. The third pile should contain the facts the student answered incorrectly. Continue to reassess the facts with each student until all of the cards are placed into the first pile. (Please note that the following cards are only a representation of the addition and subtraction facts within five. Not all facts are included.)

0 + 0 **A**	0 + 2 **B**
0 + 4 **C**	1 + 0 **D**
1 + 1 **E**	1 + 2 **F**
1 + 3 **G**	1 + 4 **H**

2 + 1 **I**	2 + 2 **J**
3 + 0 **K**	3 + 2 **L**
4 + 1 **M**	5 + 0 **N**
5 − 0 **O**	5 − 1 **P**
5 − 2 **Q**	5 − 3 **R**

5 – 4 **S**	5 – 5 **T**
4 – 1 **U**	4 – 2 **V**
4 – 3 **W**	3 – 1 **X**
3 – 2 **Y**	2 – 0 **Z**
2 – 1 **AA**	1 – 1 **AB**

Addition and Subtraction within Five

Solve.

1. $0 + 0 =$	$1 + 1 =$	$3 - 0 =$
2. $3 - 2 =$	$0 + 1 =$	$1 + 2 =$
3. $4 - 2 =$	$3 + 2 =$	$0 + 2 =$
4. $1 + 3 =$	$0 + 3 =$	$5 - 1 =$
5. $0 + 4 =$	$1 + 4 =$	$2 - 0 =$
6. $3 + 1 =$	$0 + 5 =$	$2 + 1 =$
7. $4 - 3 =$	$1 - 0 =$	$5 - 3 =$

Continue the pattern.

♡ ○ ♡ ○ ♡ ○ _____ _____

▯–▭–▯–▭–▯–▭–▯ _____ _____

A

Continue the pattern.

☐ ☐ △ ☐ ☐ △ ☐ ☐ △ _____ _____

○ ● ○ ○ ○ ● ○ ○ ● ○ _____ _____

B

How many more makes 7? Draw. Write the number.

_____ more

C

Draw circles to show 3 + 4 = 7.

D

Jane found 3 shells. Then, she found 2 more. How many shells did she find in all?

_____

E

Use two colors to color each set of cubes a different way.

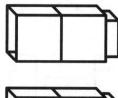

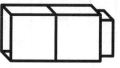

F

There are five ways to make 4. Write the number sentences.

___ + ___ = 4   ___ + ___ = 4

___ + ___ = 4   ___ + ___ = 4

___ + ___ = 4

G

Draw more triangles to make 10. Write the number.

_____ more

H

Solve.

2 + 3 = _____   1 + 1 = _____

0 + 4 = _____   2 + 2 = _____

1 + 3 = _____   4 + 1 = _____

I

Solve.

5 − 1 = _____   2 − 0 = _____

4 − 2 = _____   5 − 3 = _____

4 − 1 = _____   5 − 4 = _____

J

Name _____ Date _____

1. How many ones are in 10? Draw them.

2. Draw 10 seeds in the box on the left. Draw 5 seeds in the box on the right.

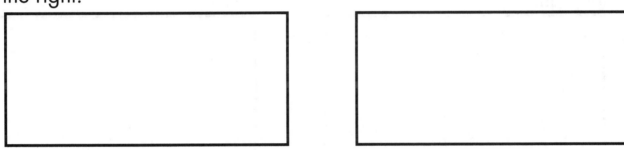

How many seeds in all? _____

3. Draw 14 crayons. Circle a set of 10. How many are left? _____

4. Greg has 10 baseballs. He wants to have 11. How many more does he need? _____

5. $10 +$ _____ $= 18$ **6.** $10 +$ _____ $= 19$

Name _____ Date _____

✦ Show What You Know ✦
Number and Operations in Base Ten

1. How many tens and ones are in 14? Draw them.

2. Draw 10 balls in the box on the left. Draw 6 balls in the box on the right.

How many balls in all? _____

3. Draw 19 oranges. Circle a set of 10. How many are left? _____

4. Penny has 10 ribbons. Her mom gives her 7 more. How many ribbons does she have now? _____

5. 10 + _____ = 11

6. 10 + _____ = 15

Name _____ Date _____

Composing and Decomposing 11 to 19

Draw a picture to show how many. Use the picture to answer the questions.

1. Holly plays with clay. She rolls 10 balls. Then, she rolls 2 more.

2. Circle the related fact for problem 1.

$$10 + 4 \qquad\qquad 10 + 3 \qquad\qquad 10 + 2$$

3. How many clay balls does Holly have in all? _____

4. John plays with clay too. He rolls 10 balls. Then, he rolls 4 more.

5. Circle the related fact for problem 4.

$$10 + 4 \qquad\qquad 10 + 9 \qquad\qquad 10 + 6$$

6. How many clay balls does John have in all? _____

7. Ivan plays with clay too. He rolls 10 balls. Then, he rolls 3 more. Write the related fact.

_____ + _____ = _____

Name _____ Date _____

Composing and Decomposing 11 to 19

Look at the ten frames. Write how many tens and ones. Write the number.

1.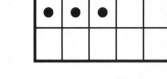

= _____ ten and _____ ones = _____

2.

= _____ ten and _____ ones = _____

3.

= _____ ten and _____ ones = _____

Show each number on the ten frames. Write how many tens and ones.

4. 18 = _____ ten + _____ ones   **5.** 12 = _____ ten + _____ ones

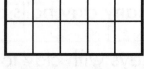
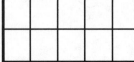
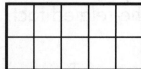

Name _____ Date _____

Composing and Decomposing 11 to 19

Solve. Draw a picture to help you.

1. You have 10 pencils but your teacher wants you to have 11. How many more pencils do you need?

_____ pencil

2. You have 10 erasers but you want to give your friend 12. How many more erasers do you need?

_____ erasers

3. You have 10 pieces of gum but your friend wants 17. How many more pieces of gum do you need?

_____ pieces of gum

4. You have 14 cars but you give your brother 10 of them. How many cars do you have left?

_____ cars

5. You have 18 markers but your sister needs to borrow 8 of them. How many markers do you have left?

_____ markers

Circle the fact that equals 18.

10 + 7

10 + 8

10 + 0

A

Circle the fact that equals 15.

10 + 3

10 + 5

10 + 8

B

The number 19 is made of 10 and 9. Write the fact.

C

The number 14 is made of 10 and 4. Write the fact.

D

Write the missing number.

_____ + 7 = 17

_____ + 9 = 19

_____ + 3 = 13

E

Write the missing number.

10 + _____ = 13

10 + _____ = 17

10 + _____ = 18

F

Name _____   Date _____

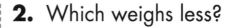

✦ Show What You Know ✦
Measurement and Data

Circle the answer to each question.

1. Which weighs more?

2. Which weighs less?

3. Which is longer?

4. Which is shorter?

5. Who is taller?

6. Which is bigger?

7. What day of the week is today?

_____

8. Draw a big heart. Draw a little heart. Circle the little heart.

9. Draw a big sun. Draw a little sun. Circle the big sun.

10. Circle the fruits.

How many pieces of fruit are there? _____

✦ Show What You Know ✦
Measurement and Data

Circle the answer to each question.

1. Which weighs more?

2. Which weighs less?

3. Which is longer?

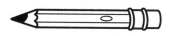

4. Which is taller?

5. Who is shorter?

6. Which is smaller?

7. What is today's date?

_____

8. Draw a big square. Draw a little square. Circle the little square.

9. Draw a big face. Draw a little face. Circle the big face.

10. Color the birds blue.

How many birds are there? _____

Name _____ Date _____

Days and Months

Use the word banks to answer the questions.

Friday	Monday	Saturday	Sunday
Thursday	Tuesday	Wednesday	

1. How many days are in a week?

6   7   10

2. Which two days make a weekend?

Saturday   Thursday   Sunday

3. Write the five days you go to school.

_____ _____ _____

_____ _____

4. What day of the week is today? _____

April	August	December	February	January	July
June	March	May	November	October	September

5. How many months are in a year?   5   9   12

6. What is the first month of the year? _____

7. What is the last month of the year? _____

8. What month is it now? _____

Name _____ Date _____

Using a Calendar

Write the name of this month at the top. Write the days of the week. Fill in the numbers.

_____

1. What day of the week is the 11th? _____

2. How many days does this month have? _____

3. How many Mondays does this month have? _____

Name _____ Date _____

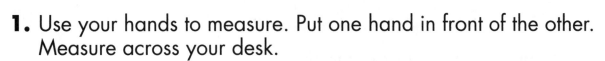

Measuring Length

1. Use your hands to measure. Put one hand in front of the other. Measure across your desk.

How many hands did it take to measure your desk? _____

2. Use your feet to measure. Put one foot in front of the other. Measure between two of your desk's legs.

How many steps did it take to measure the space? _____

3. Which is longer: your hand or your foot? _____

4. Circle the tallest tree. Color the shortest tree green.

5. Circle the longest art tool. Draw an **X** on the shortest art tool.

Measuring Weight

Use your hands to weigh objects and answer the questions.

1. Which is heavier: a pencil or a chair? _____

2. Which is lighter: a crayon box or an eraser? _____

3. What is the heaviest thing in your classroom? Draw it.

4. What is the lightest thing in your classroom? Draw it.

Draw an **H** over the heavier object. Draw an **L** over the lighter object.

5.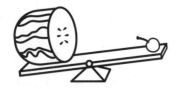

6.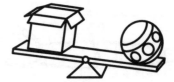

Comparing Measurements

Use the following cards as prompts for individual or group assessments. The task cards will serve as visual cues so that students can look at, weigh, or measure tangible objects in the room. Have students compare two objects and verbally describe the objects presented. You may choose to pull two cards randomly and ask, "Which is smaller?" or "Name something that weighs more." You may ask students to elaborate further and tell you how much each object may weigh, or discuss what materials the objects are made of.

chalk	marker	bulletin board
pencil	window	door
board	desk	flag

teacher's desk	a pair of shoes	poster
trash can	recycling bin	book
scissors	chair	table
eraser	crayon	paper

Comparing Measurements

Look at the objects. Circle the answer.

1. Which is longer: a pencil or an eraser?

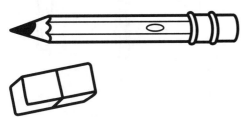

2. Which is longer: a book or a marker?

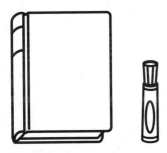

3. Which is shorter: a paper or a paper clip?

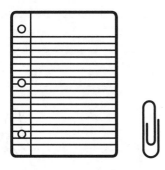

Use your hands to feel the weight of each object.

4. Which weighs less: a book or a crayon?

The _____ weighs less.

5. Which weighs more: a pencil or a coat?

The _____ weighs more.

Classifying Objects

Follow the directions to sort the items in each set.

1.

Color the drawing tools red. How many? _____

Color the other art tools blue. How many? _____

2.

Color the animals with no legs red. How many? _____

Color the animals with 2 legs blue. How many? _____

Color the animals with 4 legs green. How many? _____

3.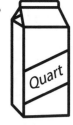

Color the drinks red. How many? _____

Color the fruits blue. How many? _____

Color the vegetables green. How many? _____

Classifying and Counting Sets

Use each set to answer the questions.

1.

How many strawberries are there? _____

How many bananas are there? _____

How many oranges are there? _____

2.

How many spoons are there? _____

How many cups are there? _____

How many forks are there? _____

3.

How many carrots are there? _____

How many heads of lettuce are there? _____

How many tomatoes are there? _____

Classifying and Sorting Objects

1. Circle the animals with wings.

2. Color the animals without wings.

3. How many animals have wings? _____

Circle each answer.

4. Which group had the least animals?

      animals with wings   animals without wings

5. Are there more cats or chickens?

           cats   chickens

A

Draw 2 things that are red.
Draw 4 things that are blue.
Color them.

Which has more? **red** **blue**

B

Draw 3 things that are yellow.
Draw 2 things that are green.
Color them.

Which has more? **yellow green**

C

Circle the object that is longer.

this paper

a crayon

D

Fill in the blanks.

A chair is taller than a

_____.

A chair is heavier than a

_____.

E

Circle the object that is longer.

a marker

a crayon

F

Circle the object that is taller.

your desk

your chair

Circle the person that is taller.

you

the teacher

Name something that is shorter than you.

_____

G

Fill in the blanks.

What is today's date?

_____

What is the date tomorrow?

_____

H

Fill in the blanks.

What day of the week is art class?

_____

In which month is Thanksgiving?

_____

I

Fill in the blanks.

_____ , Monday, Tuesday

Thursday, _____ , Saturday

March, April, _____

June, _____ , August

J

How many kids in your class are wearing blue shirts?

_____

How many kids in your class are wearing white shirts?

_____

Which group has more?

blue   white

K

How many pencils are there in your desk?

_____

How many books are there in your desk?

_____

Which group has more?

pencils   books

L

✦ Show What You Know ✦
Geometry

1. The cup is _____ the square.

below   beside   above

2. The fork is _____ the plate.

below   beside   above

3. Draw a circle.

4. Draw a triangle.

How many sides? _____

5. What is this shape? _____

How many corners? _____

6. Is this shape flat or solid?

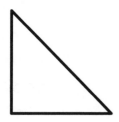
flat   solid

7. Draw lines to turn the triangle into a square.

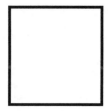

8. Draw lines to turn the square into a rectangle.

9. Is a ball a circle or a sphere?

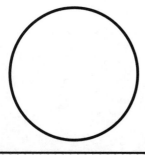
circle   sphere

10. What shape are these figures? _____

✦ Show What You Know

Geometry

1. The carrot is _____ the leaf.

         under   next to   below

2. The plate is _____ the cupcake.

         beside   under   above

3. Draw a rectangle.

4. Draw a square.

How many sides? _____

5. What is this shape? _____

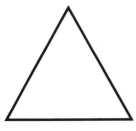

How many corners? _____

6. Is this shape flat or solid?

flat   solid

7. Draw lines to make a "T" out of the rectangle.

8. Draw lines to turn the triangle into a rectangle.

9. Is the shape of a block a square or a cube?

square   cube

10. What shape are these figures? _____

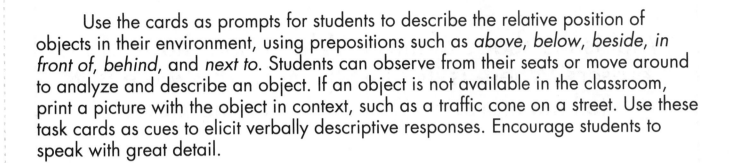

Use the cards as prompts for students to describe the relative position of objects in their environment, using prepositions such as *above*, *below*, *beside*, *in front of*, *behind*, and *next to*. Students can observe from their seats or move around to analyze and describe an object. If an object is not available in the classroom, print a picture with the object in context, such as a traffic cone on a street. Use these task cards as cues to elicit verbally descriptive responses. Encourage students to speak with great detail.

What shape is the flag? Where is it? Tell me more.	What shape is the door? Where is it? Tell me more.
What shape is the top of the desk? Where is it? Tell me more.	What is the shape of a globe? How do you know? Tell me more.
What is the shape of the book? Where is it? Tell me more.	What is the shape of the board? Where is it? Tell me more.

What is the shape of the eraser? Where is it? Tell me more.

What is the shape of the tissue box? Where is it? Tell me more.

What is the shape of a traffic cone? How do you know? Tell me more.

What is the shape of the window? Where is it? Tell me more.

What is the shape of the sheet of paper? Where is it? Tell me more.

What is the shape of a stop sign? How do you know? Tell me more.

What is the shape of the bookcase? Where is it? Tell me more.

What is the shape of a paper towel roll? How do you know? Tell me more.

Shapes in the Environment

Look around the classroom. Answer the questions.

1. Find something in the room that is a square. Draw it.

The _____ is a square.

2. Find something in the room that is a sphere. Draw it.

The _____ is a sphere.

3. Find something in the room that is a circle. Draw it.

The _____ is a circle.

4. Find something in the room that is a cube. Draw it.

The _____ is a cube.

Naming Shapes and Dimensionality

Circle to tell whether each object is a flat or solid shape.

1.
flat

solid

2.
flat

solid

3.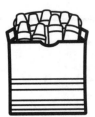
flat

solid

4.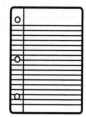
flat

solid

5.
flat

solid

6.
flat

solid

7.
flat

solid

8.
flat

solid

Name _____ Date _____

Naming Shapes and Dimensionality

1. What is this shape? _____

2. Is a cube flat or solid? _____

3. Draw a cube.

4. What is this shape? _____

5. Is a square flat or solid? _____

6. Draw a square.

Shape Attributes

1. Match the shape to its name.

cube

triangle

sphere

cylinder

hexagon

cone

square

rectangle

circle

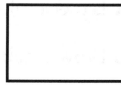

Tell how many sides and corners each shape has.

2. triangle

_____ sides

_____ corners

3. hexagon

_____ sides

_____ corners

4. rectangle

_____ sides

_____ corners

5. cube

_____ sides

_____ corners

6. cylinder

_____ sides

_____ corners

7. sphere

_____ sides

_____ corners

2-D and 3-D Shapes

Use these cards to assess students' ability to identify attributes of figures and similarities and differences between flat and solid shapes. Ask students to identify the attributes of a single shape, or present two cards for students to compare two shapes at once. Students may also sort 2-D and 3-D shapes, or compare and contrast the attributes of two shapes.

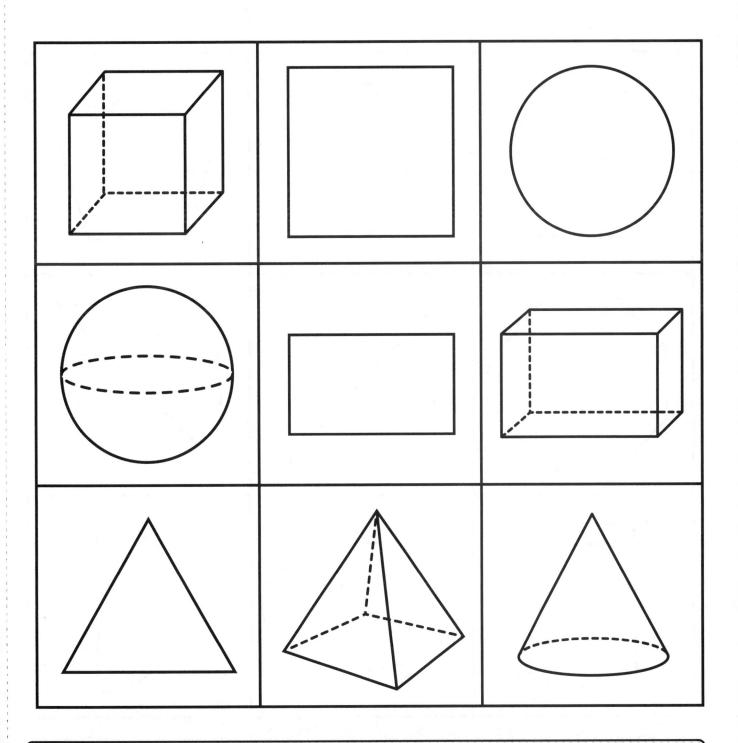

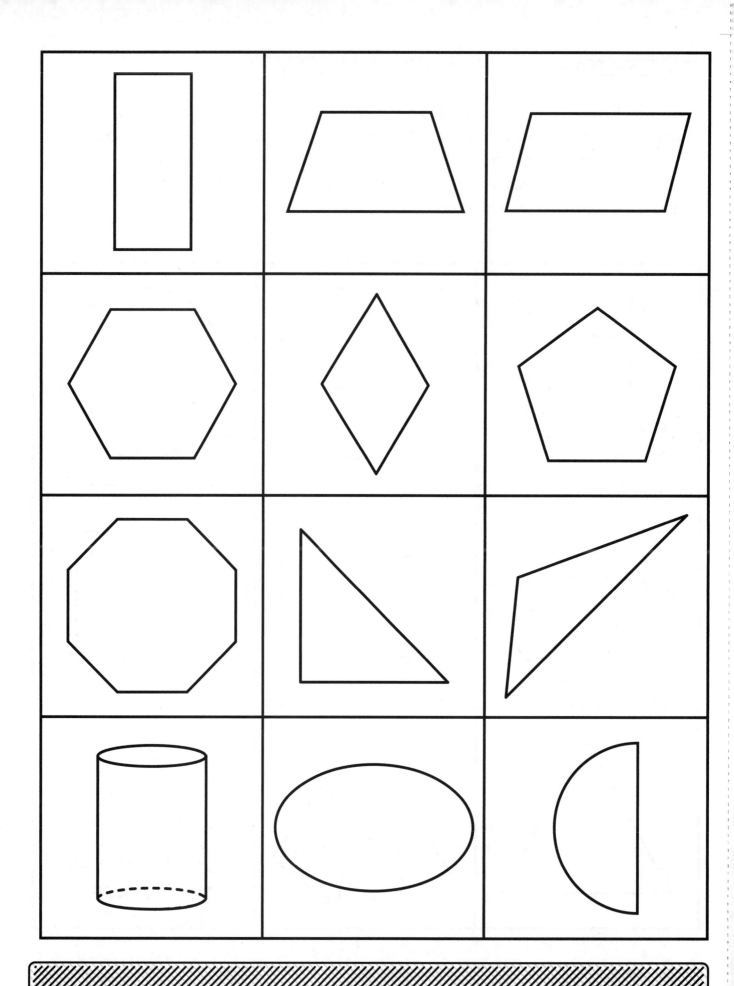

 # Composing Shapes

Use these cards as prompts to assess how a student draws, models, and builds shapes. Provide coffee stir sticks, toothpicks, or wax-covered strings, balls of clay or play dough (or marshmallows), markers, and paper to allow students to construct both flat and solid shapes. Read a card to a student, have her model the shape, and then discuss the shape by asking about its attributes. Or, have her build a shape and ask her to add to it to create a different shape.

Build a triangle. **A**	Build a square. **B**	Build a rectangle. **C**
Build a circle. **D**	Build a hexagon. **E**	Build a cube. **F**
Build a pyramid. **G**	Build a cone. **H**	Build a cylinder. **I**

Composing Shapes

Use each set of shapes to draw a new shape.

1.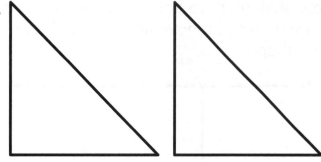

2.

3.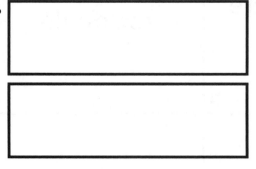

4.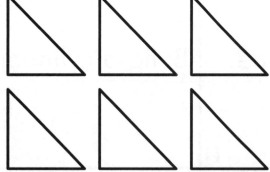

What is this shape? _____

What object has a square shape?

_____

A

What is this shape? _____

What object has a sphere shape?

_____

B

How are a diamond and a rhombus the same?

_____

_____

C

Draw a flat shape.

D

Draw a solid shape.

E

Find a rectangle in your class. Draw it.

A _____ is a rectangle.

F

Find a triangle in your class.
Draw it.

A _____ is a triangle.

G

How are a cube and a square the same?

_____
_____

H

How are a triangle and a pyramid different?

_____
_____

I

Draw a hexagon.

A hexagon has _____ sides.
A hexagon has _____ corners.

J

Draw a rectangle.

A rectangle has _____ sides.
A rectangle has _____ corners.

K

Draw a shape with 4 sides.

L

Answer Key

Pages 11–12

1. 3, 7, 12, 17, 20, 25, 31, 38, 44, 47; 2. 20, 40, 70; 3. 0, 1, 2, 3, 4, 5, 6, 7, 8, 9, 10; 4. 1, 2, 3, 4, 5; 5; 5. 14; 6. 2; 7. 6 toys; 8. 6, 10, 17

Pages 13–14

1. 2, 5, 8, 11, 14, 17, 23, 26, 29, 40, 43, 47, 54, 63, 68; 2. 30, 60, 80; 3. 0, 1, 2, 3, 4, 5, 6, 7, 8, 9, 10, 11, 12, 13, 14, 15, 16, 17, 18, 19, 20; 4. 1, 2, 3, 4, 5, 6; 6; 5. 12; 6. 3; 7. 10 cars; 8. 3, 8, 9

Page 18

1. 3, 5, 10, 12, 23, 27, 30, 34, 41, 46, 53, 60, 64, 68, 71, 76, 82, 84, 89, 95; 2. Check students' work. 3. 12, 13, 14, 15, 16; 4. 38, 39, 40, 41, 42; 5. 2, 3, 4, 5, 6

Page 21

1. 16; 2. 4; 3. 13; 4. 9; 5. Answers will vary.

Page 22

1. Check students' work. 2. 14, 17

Page 23

1–4. Answers will vary.

Page 24

1. 10 hearts; 2. 15 squares; 3. 13 circles; 4. 16 apples; 5. 19 diamonds; 6. 14 triangles; 7. 9 dots; 8. 12 stars

Page 25

1. 4; 2. 9; 3. X (equal); 4. 0; 5. 1; 6. 12; 7. X (equal); 8. 6; 9. 9; 10. 17

Page 26

1. 15 circles; 2. 12 triangles; 3. 7 diamonds; 4. 9; 5. 8

Pages 27–28

A. 4, 8; 2, 5; B. Check students' work. C. 1, 2, 3, 4, 5; 5, 6, 7, 8, 9; D–F. Check students' work. G. 10; H. 5; I. 12; J. 10; K. 5; L. 17 stars

Pges 29–30

1. 6 dots; Check students' work. 2. 5 + 5 = 10; 3. 6 – 2 = 4; 4. Check students' work. 3; 5. 2 + 3, 1 + 4; 6. 4 + 3, 6 + 1; 7. Check students' work. 3; 8. Check students' work. 6

Answer Key

Pages 31–32
1. 3 carrots; Check students' work.
2. 3 + 6 = 9; 3. 9 – 2 = 7;
4. Check students' work. 8;
5. 3 + 2, 0 + 5; 6. 6 + 3,
1 + 8; 7. Check students' work. 5;
8. Check students' work. 4

Page 33
1–5. Check students' work.

Page 34
1. 5 + 3 = 8; 2. 8 + 2 = 10;
3. 3 + 6 = 9; 4. 5 – 1 = 4;
5. 8 – 1 = 7

Pages 35–38
A. 8; B. 10; C. 10; D. 6; E. 4;
F. 6; G. 7 fingers; H. 5 fingers;
I. 8 fingers; J. 7 fingers;
K. 4 fingers; L. 4 fingers;
M. 6 shells; N. 7 frogs; O. 9 rocks;
P. 6 birds; Q. 4 ducks;
R. 0 ladybugs; S. 6 friends;
T. 8 spiders; U. 10 flowers;
V. 5 clouds; W. 4 lollipops;
X. 4 balls; Y. 2 hands; Z. 3 steps;
AA. 7 taps; AB. 8 claps;
AC. 4 taps; AD. 4 times

Page 39
1. 9 toys; 2. 3 snacks; 3. 4 times;
4. 8 socks

Page 40
1. 2 boats; 2. 5 bananas;
3. 5 trucks; 4. 2 books

Page 41
1. Check students' work. Cubes
should show 3 + 0, 0 + 3, 2 + 1,
and 1 + 2. 2. Check students'
work. Cubes should show 4 + 0,
0 + 4, 1 + 3, 3 + 1, and 2 + 2.

Page 42
Check students' work. Facts should
include 7 + 0, 0 + 7, 1 + 6, 6 + 1,
5 + 2, 2 + 5, 3 + 4, and 4 + 3.

Page 43
1. 3, 2, 5; 2. 2, 5, 7; 3. 4, 4, 4;
4. X: 3 + 4, 2 + 3, 4 + 1; 5. Check
students' work.

Page 44
Check students' work. 1. 5; 2. 4;
3. 6; 4. 7; 5. 2

Page 45
1. 5; 2. 3; 3. 6; 4. 9; 5. 10; 6. 7;
7. 4; 8. 8; 9. 1; 10. 2

Page 46
1. 4; 2. 8; 3. 10; 4. 5; 5. 7; 6. 1;
7. 2; 8. 0; 9. 3; 10. 9

Answer Key

Page 47–49
A. 0; B. 2; C. 4; D. 1; E. 2; F. 3;
G. 4; H. 5; I. 3; J. 4; K. 3; L. 5;
M. 5; N. 5; O. 5; P. 4; Q. 3; R. 2;
S. 1; T. 0; U. 3; V. 2; W. 1; X. 2;
Y. 1; Z. 2; AA. 1; AB. 0

Page 50
1. 0, 2, 3; 2. 1, 1, 3; 3. 2, 5, 2;
4. 4, 3, 4; 5. 4, 5, 2; 6. 4, 5, 3;
7. 1, 1, 2

Pages 51–52
A–B. Check students' work.
C. 4; D. Check students' work.
E. 5 shells; F. 0 + 2, 2 + 0, 1 + 1;
G. 0 + 4, 4 + 0, 1 + 3, 3 + 1,
2 + 2; H. Check students' work. 3;
I. 5, 2, 4, 4, 4, 5; J. 4, 2, 2,
2, 3, 1

Page 53
1. Check students' work. 10 ones;
2. Check students' work. 15;
3. Check students' work. 4;
4. 1 baseball; 5. 8; 6. 9

Page 54
1. Check students' work. 1 ten,
4 ones; 2. Check students' work.
16; 3. Check students' work. 9;
4. 17 ribbons; 5. 1; 6. 5

Page 55
1. Check students' work. 2. 10 + 2;
3. 12; 4. Check students' work.
5. 10 + 4; 6. 14; 7. 10 + 3 = 13

Page 56
1. 1, 3, 13; 2. 1, 7, 17; 3. 1, 5,
15; 4. 1, 8, Check students' work.
5. 1, 2, Check students' work.

Page 57
1. 1; 2. 2; 3. 7; 4. 4; 5.10

Page 58
A. 10 + 8; B. 10 + 5;
C. 10 + 9 = 19; D. 10 + 4 = 14;
E. 10, 10, 10; F. 3, 7, 8

Pages 59–60
1. cupcake; 2. leaf; 3. spoon;
4. plate; 5. child on the right;
6. dot on the left; 7. Answers will
vary. 8–9. Check students' work.
10. Check students' work. 7

Pages 61–62
1. desk; 2. mouse; 3. pencil;
4. house; 5. kid ont he right; 6. star
on the right; 7. Answers will vary.
8–9. Check students' work.
10. Check students' work. 6

Answer Key

Page 63

1. 7; 2. Saturday, Sunday;
3. Monday, Tuesday, Wednesday, Thursday, Friday; 4. Answers will vary. 5. 12; 6. January;
7. December; 8. Answers will vary.

Page 64

Check students' work.
1–3. Answers will vary.

Page 65

1–3. Answers will vary. 4. Check students' work. 5. circled: marker, X: crayon

Page 66

1. chair; 2. scissors; 3–4. Answers will vary. 5. H: watermelon, L: cherry; 6. H: ball, L: box

Page 69

1. pencil; 2. book; 3. paper clip; 4. crayon; 5. coat

Page 70

1. Check students' work. 4, 3;
2. Check students' work. 3, 5, 1;
3. Check students' work. 2, 5, 3

Page 71

1. 4, 3, 2; 2. 5, 4, 7; 3. 4, 5, 7

Page 72

1–2. Check students' work. 3. 4;
4. animals without wings;
5. chickens

Pages 73–74

A. Check students' work. blue;
B. Check students' work. yellow;
C–D. Answers will vary. E. marker;
F. chair; G. teacher, Answers will vary. H. Answers will vary.
I. Answers will vary. November;
J. Sunday, Friday, May, July;
K–L. Answers will vary.

Pages 75–76

1. above; 2. beside; 3. Check students' work. 4. Check students' work. 3; 5. square, 4; 6. solid;
7–8. Check students' work.
9. sphere; 10. circle

Pages 77–78

1. next to; 2. under; 3. Check students' work. 4. Check students' work. 4; 5. triangle, 3; 6. solid;
7–8. Check students' work.
9. cube; 10. square

Page 81

1–4. Answers will vary. Check students' work.

Answer Key

Page 82

1. solid; 2. flat; 3. solid; 4. flat;
5. solid; 6. solid; 7. flat; 8. solid

Page 83

1. cube; 2. solid; 3. Check
students' work. 4. square; 5. flat;
6. Check students' work.

Page 84

1. Check students' work. 2. 3, 3;
3. 6, 6; 4. 4, 4; 5. 6, 8; 6. 2, 0;
7. 0, 0

Page 88

1–4. Check students' work.

Pages 89–90

A. square, Answers will vary.
B. sphere, Answers will vary.
C. Answers will vary but may
include that they have four sides
and are not square. D–E. Check
students' work. F–G. Check
students' work. Answers will vary.
H. Answers will vary but may
include that a cube has square
sides. I. Answers will vary but may
include that a pyramid is solid.
J. Check students' work. 6, 6;
K. Check students' work. 4, 4;
L. Check students' work.

Notes